LOUISIANA COLONIALS: SOLDIERS AND VAGABONDS

LOUISIANA COLONIALS:

SOLDIERS AND VAGABONDS

Translated and compiled by

WINSTON DE VILLE

CLEARFIELD COMPANY

Genealogical Publishing Co., Inc.
Baltimore, Maryland
1963

Reprinted for
Clearfield Company, Inc. by
Genealogical Publishing Co., Inc.
Baltimore, Maryland
1995

International Standard Book Number: 0-8063-0094-9

The originals of these documents
are deposited in the Archives des
Colonies, in Paris. Transcripts
are in the Library of Congress
catalogued F5 B, 37.

Printed in the United States of America

Other books by

Winston De Ville

Marriage Contracts of the Opelousas Post, 1766-1803 (Co-author)

Marriage Contracts of Natchitoches, 1739-1803

Calendar of Louisiana Colonial Documents

Colonial Louisiana Marriage Contracts: Volume III and IV

To my ancestors—

soldiers and vagabonds

CONTENTS

INTRODUCTION

This book has a two-fold purpose. Primarily it should serve as a tool for Louisiana historians to weave into the written history of the colonial province the threads of detail and statistics so often lacking in some standard works. Social strata are indicated in these documents, places of origin in France, and occupations; all these factors were evidenced in the development of the colony and serious studies based on these and similar records would be a welcomed addition to the historiography of the period.

The states of Louisiana, Mississippi, and Alabama have been remarkable for the vacuity of printed sources relating to the genealogy of their colonial periods. To lessen this dearth of sources is the second purpose of this book.

To the readers of this type of publication, phrases relating these documents to the history of the area would necessarily appear sketchy. Those wishing to augment their knowledge in this field are referred to Walter Hart Blumenthal's <u>Brides</u> <u>from</u> <u>Bridewell</u> (Charles E. Tuttle Company, Rutland, Vermont, 1962), Emile Lauvriere's <u>His-</u><u>toire</u> <u>de</u> <u>la</u> <u>Louisiane</u> <u>Francaise</u> (Louisiana State University Press, Baton Rouge, 1940), and <u>La</u> <u>Louisiane</u> <u>sous</u> <u>la</u> <u>Compagnie</u> <u>des</u> <u>Indes</u> by Pierre Heinrich (Paris, 1907).

There are no special instructions for the use of this book. The title of each section indicates ports of embarkation, ships, and dates. Names are arranged in order as they appear in the original documents, while details are inserted in brief form: age, place of origin, height, color of hair, and occupation. The index is comprehensive.

The compiler gratefully acknowledges the Mobile Public Library and that institution's director, Guenter Jansen, for encouraging this and similar projects.

Winston De Ville
Head, Special Collections
Mobile Public Library

Mobile, Alabama
September 8, 1963

LOUISIANA COLONIALS:

SOLDIERS AND VAGABONDS

DESCRIPTIONS OF THE SOLDIERS OF THE NEW
RECRUITMENT OF THE COMPANY OF THE WEST
WHO EMBARKED ON THE SHIP <u>ST. LOUIS</u>,
COMMANDED BY MONSIEUR DU COULOMBIER.

Sergeants

LUC DU LOUVROY--Age 38, of Peronne, 5'5"*, auburn hair.

Soldiers

ANDRE JOUNEAU--Age 23, of La Chaume, 4'6", auburn hair.

JEAN MICHAU--Age 18, of Dejas (or Jas) in Poitou,
      4'6", auburn hair, miller.

PHILIPPE FONQUEROLLE--Age 19, of Clermont in Picardy,
      5', auburn hair, shoe-maker.

JEAN HUBERT--Age 34, of Rennes, 5'2", auburn hair,
      baker.

Prisoners sent by order of the court

ALBERT called RENCONTRE--Age 28, of Troyes in Champagne,
      5'6", black hair, hosier.

PAUL ANDRE--Age 24, of Franche Comte, 5'6", auburn
      hair.

PIERRE FRESINET--Age 27, of Grognier in Languedoc,
      6', black hair, hatter.

PICARD--Age 28, of Uzes in Languedoc, 5'6", black
      hair, lock-smith (or metal worker).

*Note: All heights are given in French measurement.

JEAN BARRY--Age 33, of Pinormiand in Casgone, 6',
            black hair, tailor.

PIERRE CAMUZAT--Age 25, of Troyes in Champagne,
            5'6", red hair, carpenter.

FRANCOIS POUPART--Age 37, of Beaumont in the
            province of Maine, 5'6", black hair.

CHARLES ARCUS--Age 19, of Clermont in Auvergne,
            4'6", red hair, lantern-maker (or
            lamplighter).

JEAN LOUIS ACHARD--Age 20, of St. Paul deverns
            in Provence, 5'4", auburn hair.

JOSEPH POMART--Age 20, of Chalons-sur-Saine,
            5'3", auburn hair.

JOSEPH JONNAN (or JOMAN or JOUNAN)--Age 20,
            of Lyon, 5', auburn hair.

FRANCOIS CATINOY--Age 20, of Franche Comte,
            5'3", black hair.

CLAUDE NICOLAS--Age 19, of Franche Comte,
            5'2", blond hair.

JEAN BAPTISTE EVRARD--Age 28, of Besancon, 5',
            auburn hair.

LA VIGNE--Age 21, of Rouen, 5'6", auburn hair,
            tailor.

TRANCHEMONTAGNE--Age 30, of Perigordin, 5'4", black
              hair, carpenter.

PRINTEMS--Age 30, of Besselier in Poitou, 6', auburn
              hair.

LA VARETTE--Age 22, of St. Antony, 5', auburn hair,
              weaver.

Additions

VINCENT MICHEL ROUSSELET--Age 18, of St. Jean d'Angely,
              5', auburn hair.

JOSEPH ROUSSELET--Age 16, of St. Jean d'Angely, 5',
              auburn hair.

Soldiers

SIMON LE GENDRE--Age 38, of Passy near Paris, 5'2",
              auburn hair, carpenter.

SIMON FOUQUET (DE BELLECOURT ?)--(Of Bellecourt ?),
              sent from Paris.

1719

DESCRIPTIONS OF THE SOLDIERS OF THE NEW RECRUITMENT OF THE COMPANY OF THE WEST WHO EMBARKED ON THE FLUTE DAUPHINE, COMMANDED BY MONSIEUR DE LA FEUILLEE.

Sergeant

JACQUES LE VILLAIN, SIEUR DE BEAUMENAL--Age 45, of Alencon, 5', blond hair.

Soldiers

CARLIER--Age 38, of Chateauroux, 5', auburn hair.

JEAN LIZEUX--Age 23, of Angoumois (or Dangoumois), 5'2", black hair, lock-smith (or metal worker).

RENE LE COURT--Age 18, of Niort, 5'2", black hair, lock-smith (or metal worker).

LA MOTHE HERMIES (or HERMIET)--Age 27, of Rennes, 5', black hair, wig-maker or barber.

PIERRE FUYER--Age 19, of Angers, 5'3", auburn hair, dyer (tinturier).

JEAN HENAULT--Age 28, of La Fond near La Rochelle, 5', auburn hair, cooper.

JEAN ROBIN--Age 17, of Charente, 4'6", auburn hair.

FRANCOIS NICOLAS DUHAMEL--Age 22, of St. Donnatien
        Parish in Paris, 5', auburn hair.

JEAN LE COQ--Age 28, of Contances, 5'4", auburn hair,
        cook.

PIERRE SIMONNET--Age 19, of Soudan Parish of St.
        Messan, 5', black hair, weaver.

OLLIVIER EVENAN--Age 21, of Bretagne, 5'2", auburn
        hair, marshal (marechal).

CLAUDE METAYER--Age 32, of Pontivy in Bretagne, 5',
        auburn hair, baker.

JEAN BRUNET--Age 29, of Saumur, 5', black hair, weaver.

CHARLES CASMIER--Age 22, of Preseilly (or Preuilly)
        in Touraine, 5', black hair.

PIERRE HENRY--Age 24, of Montauban, 5', black hair,
        tailor.

PIERRE HOCART--Age 28, of Tours, 4'6", black hair,
        cadet.

COURBINET DE BILLIEUX--Age 27, of Vitre in Bretagne,
          5', auburn hair, cadet.

JOUBART--Age 23, of Paris, 4'6", auburn hair, cadet.

Prisoners sent from Lyon

CLAUDE AUDIN VALENTIN--Age 35, of St. Didier in Vellay,
          5', black hair, mason.

ETIENNE QUINAU called COUCOU--Age 22, of Morvan in
          Lyonnais, 5'2", auburn hair, hatter.

GERARD MARCIER--Age 23, of Bonne in Bourgogne, 5'2",
          auburn hair, mason.

JEAN PRIEUR--Age 35, of Interville in Champagne,
          5'2", grey hair.

FLEURY HASSY (or HAFY)--Age 17, of St. Germy in Forest,
          4'6", auburn hair.

FRANCOIS DARBET--Age 20, of Lyon, 5', auburn hair.

JACQUES ROUANNE--Age 25, of Mortagne in Perche, 4'6",
          auburn hair.

FRANCOIS RAMBAULT--Age 22, of Bussan in Dauphine,
        5'5", auburn hair, laborer.

JEAN LAVENOT--Age 22, of Cap in Dauphine, 5'5",
        auburn hair.

ANTOINE DURAND--Age 23, of Lyon, 5', auburn hair,
        shoe-maker.

JEAN GUAY--Age 18, of Bresle in the diocese of Lyon,
        auburn hair.

JEAN BAPTISTE PIPI

JOSEPH CLERY called SANSOUCY

DESTOURETTES--Age 26, of La Rochelle, 4'6", black
        hair.

DESCRIPTIONS OF THE SOLDIERS OF THE NEW
RECRUITMENT OF THE COMPANY OF THE WEST
WHO EMBARKED ON THE FLUTE <u>MARIE</u>, COM-
MANDED BY MONSIEUR <u>JAPYE</u>.

<u>Sergeants</u>

GUERIN--Age 40, of Paris, 5', auburn hair.

GARNIER--Age 28, of Blois, 5'7", auburn hair.

GIBERTY--Age 27, of Luxembourg, 5'7", blond hair.

<u>Corporal</u>

VINCENT--Age 38, of Paris, 5', auburn hair.

<u>Cadets</u>

FRANCOIS SOYER--Age 17, of Brie, 4'4", auburn hair.

CHARLES BONTEMS--Age 18, of St. Cloud, 4'6", blond
hair.

Soldiers

JEAN GENTIL--Age 19, of Rochefort, 5', blond hair, tailor.

EDME VISTARD--Age 30, of Auxerre in Bourgogne, 4'6", blond
        hair, hosier.

JEAN BUFFY--Age 20, of Saisiere in the bishopric of
        Laon, 5', black hair.

CHARLES DIETTE--Age 21, of Disoudun in Berie, 4'8",
        auburn hair, barber or wig-maker.

JEAN BEAUVAIS--Age 17, of Bourg-sur-Garonne, 5', auburn
        hair, marshal (marechal).

CHARLES VOLART--Age 29, of Grisy in Normandy, 5', auburn
        hair.

MICHEL MICHIN--Age 20, of Cognac, 5'2", auburn hair,
        laborer.

FRANCOIS LE DE--Age 19, of St. Brieux in Bretagne, 5',
        auburn hair, marshal (marechal).

BARTHELEMY DE LA HAYE--Age 19, of Paris, 5', auburn hair,
        harness-maker.

PIERRE LA MOTHE--Age 21, of Vienne in Bourbonnois, 5',
blond hair.

PIERRE SORET--Age 22, of Richelieu in Poitou, 5', black
hair, laborer.

JEAN MARGUET--Age 18, of Chateauneuf in Normandy, 5'2",
black hair, shoe-maker.

FRANCOIS BALAY--Age 22, of Amber in Auvergne, 5'2",
auburn hair, perfumer.

NICOLAS BLERET--Age 26, of Bourgogne, 5'4", auburn hair,
laborer.

ROGUES MICHEL--Age 26, of St. Sulpice parish in Paris,
5', auburn hair.

LOUIS DU MONT--Age 38, of Chaulons in Bourgogne, 5'2",
auburn hair.

JEAN CLAUTIER--Age 27, of Pate in Chartres, 5', auburn
hair, laborer.

CHRISTOPHE MAINNARD--Age 20, of Curzon in Poitou, 5'4",
auburn hair.

LOUIS DU PAIN--Age 18, of Saine in Poitou, 5', auburn
          hair, cooper.

PIERRE PAVILS--Age 16, of Rheins in Champagne, 4'10",
          auburn hair, shoe-maker.

NICOLAS FLERIEUX--Age 21, of Langres in Champagne, 5',
          auburn hair, cutler.

PIERRE LE ROY--Age 18, of Rheims in Champagne, 5',
          auburn hair, mason.

ROBERT DE LA HAYE--Age 21, of Cheauthiery, 5'4", auburn
          hair.

JEAN JOLLIN--Age 26, of Niort, 5'6", auburn hair,
          laborer.

JEAN MARCHAND--Age 20, of Rennes in Bretagne, 5'2",
          auburn hair, weaver.

CLAUDE BENOIST--Age 35, of St. Martin La Fosse, 4'6",
          black hair, laborer.

FRANCOIS DU MONT--Age 29, of Chaulons in Bourgogne, 5',
          auburn hair.

LOUIS LA MARCHE--Age 22, of Monfort in Maine, 4'8", auburn
          hair, laborer.

RENE GAULTIER--Age 18, of St. Hilaire in Normandy, 4',
auburn hair, laborer.

FRANCOIS GENTIL--Age 25, of Serie near Orleans, 4'6",
black hair, butcher.

LOUIS RAYMOND BOILEDIEU--Age 35, of Sivray in Poitou,
5'1", black hair, <u>fendeur</u> <u>de</u> <u>merain</u>.

MILAN DENIS--Age 30, of Chaguy in Bourgogne, 4', black
hair, carpenter.

JEAN BAPTISTE BOQUET--Age 22, of Chartre in Bosse, 5',
auburn hair, cooper.

LOUIS MICHELET--Age 21, of Lance in Picardy, 5',
auburn hair.

<u>Deserters</u> <u>and</u> <u>others</u> <u>sent</u> <u>by</u> <u>order</u> <u>of</u> <u>the</u> <u>king</u>

MICHEL BEAU--Age 30, of Piege, 5'2", black hair, tailor.

FRANCOIS CHARPENTIER--Age 22, of Justinie, 5'1", auburn
hair, laborer.

PIERRE LAURENDICQ called CHEVALIER--Age 21, of Chermiche(?),
5'2", auburn hair, draper or clothier.

JEAN PIERRE BONGER--Age 20, of Venise, 5'1", black hair.

GEORGES CLARASKY called LA VIOLETTE--Age 23, of Otratte,
        5'5", auburn hair, lock-smith (or metal
        worker).

BENOIST MONDER ST. AMANT--Age 22, of Chapeauoine, 5'2",
        auburn hair, tanner.

PIERRE LE TOURNEUR--Age 35, of Poissy, 5'2", black hair,
        butcher.

PHILIPPE STERLING--Age 27, of Alost, 5'3", black hair,
        draper or clothier.

JEAN BAPTISTE BRAU--Age 30, of Auchange (or Anchange),
        4'5", black hair, carder or wool-comber.

PIERRE PASQUIER--Age 22, of Mans, 5'2", black hair,
        weaver.

JACQUE BRIGOND BELLAIR--Age 30, of Roy in Champagne,
        4'5", black hair, carder or wool-comber.

PANERASSE HOBREMAN--Age 26, of Boylac, 4'7", black hair.

THOMAS NOORWEGH called NOORT--Age 24, from London, 5'1",
auburn hair, draper or clothier.

JEAN BOID--Age 22, from England, 4'5", auburn hair,
tinker, died of the _maladie_ on the way
(_en rade_).

FRANCOIS LONGCHAMPS--Age 24, of Orleans, 5'1", auburn
hair, joiner or carpenter.

JEAN FRANCOIS VIGNERON called LA VIOLETTE--Age 30, of
Jogny, 5'4", auburn hair.

DANIEL HIGUET--Age 30, of Ireland, 5'4", auburn hair.

JEAN BAPTISTE JARRY--Age 21, of Paris, 5', auburn hair.

JEAN SANSON DE LA GRANGE--Age 26, of Noyars, 5'3",
auburn hair, weaver.

AMBROISE MOREAU--Age 30, of Jardeton, 5'2", auburn hair.

NICOLAS LE BRETON--Age 22, of Landerneau in Bretagne, 5',
auburn hair.

JACQUES LE BOURGEOIS--Age 45, of Paris, 5'2", auburn
hair.

IGNACE DE BOLLE--Age 30, of St. Paul de Lion, 5'1",
          black hair.

ANTOINE GERRE DE LA VILLETTE--Age 23, of Paris, 5',
          auburn hair, miner.

FRANCOIS BUFFET--Age 30, of Jossy, 5'2", auburn hair,
          miller.

SIMON STELLY--Age 35, of Ambrassin, 5'2", black hair,
          miller.

ALBERT DE ST. FRONLLY--Age 26, of Pitersene, 5'4",
          auburn hair.

JACQUES CALLERY--Age 21, of Moullin, 5'2", auburn hair,
          turner.

CHRISTIAN LADNER--Age 20, of Pitersene, 5'4", auburn hair.

PIERRE BARGAU--Age 30, of Florance, 5'5", auburn hair,
          button-maker.

PIERRE FRANCOIS PETROUCHY--Age 25, of Leonce, 5'5",
          auburn hair, shoe-maker.

By order of the king

CHAVANNES--Age 35, of Paris, 4'6", black hair.

JACQUES RENAULT--Age 16, of Rouen, 4'6", auburn hair,
             barber or wig-maker.

Tobacco smugglers

DOMINIQUE REGESOULAMOTTE--Age 30, of Rennes, 5', auburn
             hair.

JULLIEN SANSOT--Age 28, of Angouleme, 4'8", auburn hair.

DESCRIPTIONS OF THE SOLDIERS OF THE NEW
RECRUITMENT OF THE COMPANY OF THE WEST
WHO EMBARKED ON THE SHIP <u>UNION</u>, COM-
MANDED BY MONSIEUR DE LA MANSELIERE
GRAVE.

Sergeant

JACQUES LIVET--Age 30, of Lyon, 5'1", blond hair, tailor.

Cadets

The <u>Sieurs</u>:

SAINTON, the elder--Age 20, of Chatellerault in Poitou,
       5'1", auburn hair.

SAINTON, the younger--Age 18, of Chatellerault in Poitou,
       5'2", auburn hair.

DARBONNE--Age 20, of Paris, 4', black hair.

MICHEL--Age 19, of Paris, 5'2", auburn hair.

MORISETTE--Age 28, of Chareux in Poitou, 5'1", black
       hair.

DU FOURG--Age 29, of.Bordeaux, 5', auburn hair.

DEY SAULTIER--Age 17, of La Rochelle, 4'6", auburn hair.

GEORGES USQUAIN--Age 17, of Douzy in Bourgogne, 5'1",
                auburn hair.

LOQUET--Age 24, of Paris, 4'6", auburn hair.

RENEUX--Age 21, of Paris, 5', auburn hair.

SANDRA--Age 19, of Paris, 4'7", auburn hair.

Soldiers

PIERRE HEROUX--Age 22, of Bellefort in Alsace, 5',
               auburn hair, butcher.

VINCENT FRANCOIS AMIET--Age 20, of Avanton near Poitiers,
               4'8", blond hair, laborer.

PIERRE JAMIN--Age 24, of Paris, 5'1", auburn hair, brush-
              maker or brush-seller.

NICOLAS BRINGUAN--Age 32, of Paris, 5', auburn hair,
                  goldsmith or silversmith.

ROBERT CHERON--Age 29, of Rouen, 5', auburn hair, (occupation illegible).

JEAN LA VERGNE--Age 19, of Chastelvent, 4'8", auburn hair, marshal (marechal).

JEAN LOUIS LOUVY--Age 20, of Paris, 5', black hair, pastry-cook.

LOUIS SALOMON--Age 31, of Mans, 5'1", auburn hair, armourer or gunsmith.

ADRIEN LE CAPITAINE--Age 25, of Normandy, 5', blond hair, cook.

JACQUES PAQUET--Age 30, of Riom in Auvergne, 5', auburn hair, barber (barbier).

GUILLAUME BARBAULT--Age 30, of Normandy, 5'6", auburn hair, blacksmith.

JACQUES CHEUVEIER--Age 23, of Paris, 5', black hair, joiner or carpenter.

PIERRE GOBET--Age 30, of Marsomain in Switzerland, 5'7", auburn hair, blacksmith.

PHILIPPE MARTEAU--Age 27, of Paris, 4'6", auburn hair, shoe-maker.

FRANCOIS PERRUCHON--Age 25, of Rennes, 5', black hair, gardener.

CHARLES CROLIES--Age 24, of Bourbonnois, 5'1", auburn hair.

FRANCOIS PATREU--Age 30, of St. Brieux in Bretagne, 5'3", black hair.

CLAUDE GOUIN--Age 41, of Angers, 5'2", black hair.

NICOLAS ROBIN--Age 23, of St. Jean la Chaisse, 5', auburn hair, mason.

Deserters

NICOLAS JOUSSAINT called LA BONTE--Age 30, of Lorraine, 5'3", auburn hair.

CLAUDE DU VAL--Age 24, of Rouen, 5'5", auburn hair.

HYACINTHE GEOFFROY called PROVENCAL--Age 20, of St. Viran(?), 5'2", auburn hair, gardener.

JOACHIM CLAUDE called SANS FACON--Age 25, of Daix, 5'4",
auburn hair.

GASPARD STOCLY--Age 28, of More, 5'2", blond hair.

JEAN GEORGE called BATAILLON--Age 29, of Montpellier,
5'4", blond hair.

GASPARD HINGLER--Age 30, of Agry, 5'2", black hair.

FRANCOIS POSSAT--Age 35, of Fribourg, 5'3", black hair.

PIERRE BIDEAUD DE ST. JACQUES--Age 28, of St. Gaultier,
5'2", black hair, laborer.

MAURICE CHERY--Age 20, of Switzerland, 5'3", black hair.

PIERRE LEONNARD DE ST. MICHEL--Age 20, of Monberon, 5'1",
black hair.

JEAN CLAUDE DE LA COUZE--Age 22, of Saonne, 5'3",
auburn hair.

JACQUES LORAIN--Age 20, of Avignon, 5'2", auburn hair.

LOUIS VINCENT THERASSE called POITTEVIN--Age 25, of Poitiers, 5'4", black hair.

CLAUDE ANTOINE PETIT--Age 25, of Vaudry, 5'4", black hair.

PASQUET DE QUESNE--Age 22, of Canda, 5'3", auburn hair.

BARTHELEMY GRANDIN DE ST. LOUIS--Age 30, of Montbasson, 4'8", auburn hair.

JEAN DESPACE called BEAUSEJOUR--Age 25, of Liege, 5'5", auburn hair.

JEAN ALMESSE DE LANGLOIS--Age 35, of London, 5'3", black hair.

ANTOINE MEDIEU called BELLE FLEUR--Age 30, of Morias, 5', auburn hair, tailor.

JACQUES JEUNE called BAGUETTE--Age 28, of Maubeuge, 5'1", auburn hair.

VINCELLE STARUSQUY--Age 35, of Ireland, 5'3", auburn hair.

ZACHARIE BEAUREPAS--Age 25, of Ireland, 5'3", auburn hair, butcher.

JEAN GUILLAUME BEURET--Age 22, of Solur, 4'6", auburn
hair, weaver.

ANTOINE GABRIEL called LA FOREST--Age 40, of St.
Clerneus(?), 5'3", auburn hair.

GASPARD SILAR--Age 30, of Switzerland, 5', auburn hair.

GERAUD VALTRE--Age 24, of Switzerland, 5'4", black hair.

CLAUDE FORTIER DE BEAULIER--Age 28, of Paris, 5'2",
black hair.

MARTIN ROSPASSER--Age 34, of Switzerland, 5'2", black
hair, tailor.

FRANCOIS ANTOINE JOSSE--Age 28, of Switzerland, 5'3",
auburn hair.

JEAN RENAULT called SANS REGRET--Age 27, of Selon, 5'2",
auburn hair.

NOEL AUBERT--Age 28, of Paris, 5'3", auburn hair.

PIERRE FRANCOIS THIBAUD called SANSQUARTIER--Age 23, of
Flanders, 5'3", blond hair.

LOUIS DAUGES called LA SONDE--Age 23, of Lyon, 5'4",
auburn hair, <u>frater</u>.

FRANCOIS DE SALLE--Age 30, of Ambersan, 5'3", black hair,
turner.

MICHEL GRONDIN--Age 22, of Mortin, 5'2", auburn hair,
marshal (<u>marechal</u>).

RENE BRINDONNEAU--Age 23, of Chausse, 5', black hair,
mason.

ANDRE PASQUIER called BEAULIEU--Age 27, of Paris, 5'1",
black hair, <u>maitre en fait d'armes</u>.

SIMON LAISNE--Age 25, of Rouen, 5'3", auburn hair,
barber (<u>barbier</u>).

MATHIEU SALOUIN called LA PRUDENCE--Age 26, of Switzerland, 5'3", auburn hair.

FRANCOIS POZAT--Age 25, of Switzerland, 5'6", black hair.

<u>Tobacco Smugglers</u>

PIERRE VOISIN called MONTREUIL--Age 30, of St. Pierre de
More, 5'4", black hair.

24

PIERRE BOUTEAU--Age 40, of Rennes, 5', black hair,
    laborer.

Dealers in contraband salt

CLAUDE GUILLAUME--Age 18, of Loan, 5', black hair.

JEAN GUILLAUME--Age 17, of Loan, 5'1", auburn hair, weaver.

PIERRE MAGNY--Age 40, of Flers, 5'1", auburn hair,
    laborer.

Vagabonds sent from Paris and other places

JEAN CHECHERY--Age 21, of Rennes, 5'5", auburn hair, miller.

CHARLES BELLAMY--Age 19, of Coustances, 5', auburn hair,
    printer.

GERMAIN CAZE--Age 26, of St. Godin, 4'4", black hair,
    brazier or coopersmith.

JEAN LAUNAY--Age 22, of Mans, 5'3", black hair, laborer.

URBAIN PAQUIOT--Age 15, of Bertinet, 4', auburn hair.

RENE AUTIN DE LA MEILLERAY--Age 20, of Molleray, 4'4",
        auburn hair.

FRANCOIS SAUSSIE--Age 18, of Rennes, 5', black hair,
        laborer.

JEAN CHENAY--Age 18, of La Fleche, 5', black hair, laborer.

PIERRE ARREAU (or ARRIAU)--Age 17, of Cormery, 4'5",
        black hair.

THOMAS DEMARS--Age 19, of La Fleche, 5', auburn hair.

PIERRE GUERARD--Age 26, of Caen, 5'1", black hair,
        laborer.

NICOLAS VALLET--Age 17, of Rennes, 4'4", auburn hair,
        laborer.

JEAN GUILLOY--Age 18, of Laval, 5'1", auburn hair,
        weaver.

JEAN BAPTISTE FERRAND--Age 22, of Sens, 5', blond hair,
        carder or wool-comber.

JEAN VENIER--Age 40, of Paris, 5'2", auburn hair.

ROBERT JUS--Age 20, of Paris, 5', black hair.

CHARLES LA COUR--Age 18, of Paris, 5', black hair,
          shoe-maker.

SIMON MENARD--Age 25, of Paris, 4'5", black hair,
          spectacle-maker or spectacle-seller.

JACQUES LAMERON--Age 22, of Garin, 5'2", auburn hair,
          tanner.

JEAN VERNAY--Age 22, of Beaume, 5'1", black hair.

ESTIENNE TOUSSIGER--Age 25, of Paris, 5', black hair,
          cook.

LOUIS BELLAR--Age 22, of Donay, 5', black hair, laborer.

GUILLAUME DEMPIERRE--Age 25, of Beauvais, 5'6", black
          hair.

JEAN CHARLES--Age 30, of Ste. Marie, 5'2", black hair.

PIERRE SENOUCHE--Age 27, of Lyon, 4'6", black hair.

DESCRIPTIONS OF THE SOLDIERS OF THE NEW
RECRUITMENT, DEALERS IN CONTRABAND SALT,
TOBACCO SMUGGLERS, DESERTERS, AND VAGA-
BONDS WHO EMBARKED ON THE SHIP DUC DE
NOAILLES, COMMANDED BY MONSIEUR COULAN,
TO SERVE IN LOUISIANA.

Sergeant

JACQUES LA ROCHE--Age 43, of Chalons in Champagne, 4'8",
black hair "pt. perruque," tailor.

Cadets

The Sieurs:

CLAUDE TILLOY--Age 21, of Paris, 5', blond hair.

ANTOINE JORDAN--Age 19, of Valence, 5'2", blond hair.

JEAN BAPTISTE MALTER--Age 18, of St. Sauveur parish in
Paris, 4'8", black hair.

Soldiers

PIERRE ANTOINE DU FLOS--Age 30, of Tournay in Flanders,
5', brown hair.

GUY LE GUERNE--Age 24, of Carhaix in Bretagne, 5'4",
              black hair.

CLAUDE MERCIER--Age 17, of Paris, 4'6", blond hair,
              tailor.

ELZEAR FELIX DE CREVECOEUR--Age 36, of St. Omer, 4'1",
              brown hair.

LUC DRUET--Age 17, of Nancy, 4', blond hair.

CLAUDE ROUSSEL--Age 44, of Corley in Picardy, 5',
              auburn hair, laborer.

DENIS GOUET--Age 20, of St. Germain de Lauxerrois parish
              in Paris, 5'2", black hair, butcher.

PIERRE VOYSIN--Age 24, of St. Sauveur parish in Paris,
              5', auburn hair, pavior.

PIERRE BEZUCHET--Age 17, of St. Sulpice parish near
              the Cherche Midy in Paris, 5', black
              hair.

FRANCOIS MOREAU--Age 33, of Chateau Signon in Guernois,
              5', black hair, worker in silk.

FRANCOIS BILLECAULT--Age 37, of Auzerre in Bourgogne,
5'2", black hair, surgeon (chirurgien).

JACQUES GOUET--Age 26, of Clermont in Auvergne, 5'2",
auburn hair, weaver.

RENE DU ROCHER--Age 16 years and 6 months, of Poitiers,
4'8", black hair, barber or wig-maker.

FLORENT LEMOINE--Age 18, of Saumur, 4'10", black hair,
barber or wig-maker.

CHARLES DU VAL--Age 24, of Villedieu in Normandy, 5',
auburn hair, surgeon (chirurgien).

FRANCOIS DU BOIS--Age 20, of St. Louis parish in Bayonne,
5'1", black hair.

LOUIS OZANNE--Age 20, of La Tardiere in the bishopric
of La Rochelle, 5'2", auburn hair.

JEAN DU PRE--Age 15, of Rochefort "de la vielle paroisse,"
5', blond hair.

AGATTE AUGE PERDON--Age 45, of Saumur, 5'2", blond hair,
surgeon (chirurgien).

FRANCOIS MAINQUENEAU--Age 21, of Paris, 5', brown hair.

JEAN MAILLARD--Age 22, of Brest in Bretagne, 5', auburn
              hair.

JEAN DE LA MARZELLE--Age 40, of Libourne, 5', black hair.

NICOLAS BREAU--Age 26, of Nevers, 5'2", black hair,
              marshal (marechal).

JEAN FRANCOIS FREMENTIER--Age 45, of Rennes, 5'2", blond
              hair.

ETIENNE LE ROY--Age 30, of La Fleche in Anjou, 5'2",
              black hair, joiner or carpenter.

Persons exiled by order of the king

Dealers in contraband salt

JEAN BRUNET--Age 19, of Angers, 5', fort clair, miller.

CHARLES CALET--Age 35, of Versan in Bourbonnois, 5'1",
              brown hair, miller.

FRANCOIS GIRAULT called BONNEMENS--Age 30, of Rilly, 5',
              black hair, vine-dresser or wine-grower.

RENE LINGER--Age 45, of Martizet, 5'1", black hair, edge-
      tool maker.

JACQUES GENTIL--Age 41, of Martizet, 5'1", black hair,
      laborer.

LOUIS PERIN--Age 42, of Reont in Poitou, 5'1", black hair,
      laborer.

ALEXIS DU JARDIN--Age 21, of Reignol, 5'1", "clair,"
      gardener.

GUILLAUME CHAPELLE--Age 48, of Ste. Marie du Bois, 5'4",
      black hair, laborer.

PIERRE MALSIEU--Age 42, of Charbain, 5' boigne,   grey
      hair, sailor.

LOUIS DE ROCHE--Age 26, of Neville in Normandy, 5'1",
      auburn hair, laborer.

CLAUDE RIDEL--Age 33, of Paris, 5'3", black hair, joiner
      or carpenter.

JEAN FROCOUR--Age 4- (possibly 45), of Amiens, 5'4",
      black hair, laborer.

JOSEPH DESCHAMPS called LA RIZE--Age 40, of Lamboy,
        5'3", black hair, rope-maker.

CLAUDE GLAINE--Age 24, of Dauphine, 5'2", "clair,"
        carpenter and wheelright.

JEAN DU PRE--Age 13, of Serreport, 4'5", "clair," shoe-
        maker.

LOUIS NICOLAS FAMECHON--Age 15, of Dinque, 4'5", blond
        hair.

LOUIS MASSUEL--Age 30, of Hotion, 5'3", auburn hair.

JACQUES BOUCHET--Age 42, of La Salle Guenant, 5'1",
        black hair, laborer.

FRANCOIS DAUPHIN--Age 32, of Reout in Poitou, 5', black
        hair.

NICOLAS PALLIER--Age 45, of Sere in Touraine, 5', auburn
        hair.

FRANCOIS BAUDET called BASTILLON--Age 48, of Chapelle
        Blanche, 5', grey hair.

LOUIS BLANCHARD--Age 15, of Arles, 4', ash-colored hair.

ADRIEN VERDURE--Age 50, of Cette Outtre, 5', ash-colored
hair.

JEAN GOTTEFRIN--Age 50, of Corbie near Amiens, 5'2",
black hair, laborer.

LOUIS ASSAY called MANCHET--Age 50, of Montrichard in
Touraine, 5', auburn hair, laborer.

PIERRE AUBERT--Age 55, of Crisse, 5'2", grey hair, mason.

VINCENT FROGET called PIED DE CHAT--Age 38, of Marseille,
5', black hair.

JEAN DE MARLY--Age 43, of Laudoussy-la-Ville, 5'1", black
hair, weaver.

LOUIS BLOCHET--Age 33, of Verlay, 5'3", auburn hair.

JEAN BAPTISTE TRINGUAR--Age 15, of Caveillan, 4'8",
"fort clair."

THOMAS DU PRE--Age 14, of Severpan, 5', black hair, shoe-
maker.

THOMAS ANSAU--Age 42, of Coutance, 5'3", black hair.

BERNARD DE VAU--Age 17, of Paris, 5'1", auburn hair,
              tanner.

ANTOINE ALLARD--Age 20, of Montreuil, 4'9", black hair.

GEORGES TESSON--Age 34, of Metz, 5', auburn hair, laborer.

JACQUES LAMBERT--Age 34, of St. Meuline, 5', black hair.

JACQUES NOIRON--Age 38, of Barenton-sur-Seine, 4'6", black
               hair.

MICHEL NOIRON--Age 38, of Rimar, 5'5", "fort clair,"
              chartier (probably carter or waggoner).

JEAN DE MARLY--Age 35, "de-mione", 5'2", "fort clair,"
              weaver.

PHILIPPE DE HAUT called ST. OLIVE--Age 30, of Corby,
               5'1", "clair."

JEAN DAUNIN--Age 37, of Neully, 5'2", black hair, weaver.

JEAN BAPTISTE MOLLARD called MONTAL--Age 31, of Paris,
   5'2", "clair," joiner or carpenter.

FRANCOIS COUTTANT--Age 38, of Tiviere, 5'3", black hair,
   expert seaman.

Tobacco Smugglers

ETIENNE MALEZIEUX--Age 47, of Dampierre in Champagne,
   4'5", auburn hair, laborer.

NICOLAS D'ESTEL--Age 24, of Metz, 5', "clair," baker.

JEAN COLLAIN--Age 30, of Coublance, 5'4", "clair,"
   rope-maker.

JEAN BIAT--Age 28, of Elbert, 4'6", black hair, brazier
   or coppersmith.

PIERRE CUSSIN--Age 33, of Sarmelieux, 5'1", black hair,
   vine-dresser or wine-grower.

PIERRE PASSERAT--Age 36, of St. Etienne in Forest, 5'2",
   black hair, gardener.

LOUIS GUERNEL--Age 18, of Rhodon, 5'3", "fort clair,"
   "chartier" laborer.

JEAN GOTTARD--Age 27, of Lyon, 5'1", blond hair, weaver.

ENNEMOND BERSON--Age 50, of Lyon, 4'5", "fort clair,"
            laborer.

PIERRE MAURIX--Age 30, of Marsoninge in Bresse, 5',
            "fort clair," laborer.

JOSEPH JOUNNAS--Age 30, of "la voute de vantadouce,"
            5'2", "fort clair," tailor.

LAURENS FERRAND--Age 50, of Confrainchon, 5'1", "fort
            clair," laborer.

FRANCOIS CHERON--Age 34, of Bordeaux, 5', auburn hair.

LOUIS ROUSSEL--Age 16, of Langre, 5', auburn hair,
            laborer.

BENOIST ETIENNE VEILLON--Age 35, of Lyon, 4'5", auburn
            hair, chartier.

CLAUDE DU TARTRE--Age 25, of Franche Comte, 5'1",
            auburn hair, miller.

JEAN SOUBAYGNE--Age 34, of Dax, 5', black hair.

CLAUDE BERNARD called CHAMBERY--Age 27, "du d. Lieu,"
    5'2", auburn hair, laborer.

FRANCOIS BERTHELOT called MARIAS--Age 48, of Talont,
    4'8", black hair, expert seaman.

JOSEPH RAFFIN--Age 40, of Curtia, 5'6", auburn hair,
    miller.

ANTOINE FLEURY--Age 32, of Bourg in Bresse, 5'6", auburn
    hair.

Vagabonds taken at Orleans

SILVAIN THOMAS--Age 35, of Meule, 4'7", black hair,
    laborer.

PIERRE FAUSSET--Age 23, of Jussy in Brie, 4'7", black
    hair, laborer.

MICHEL BRANCHET--Age 54, of St. Benoist-sur-Loire, 5'2",
    grey hair, laborer.

ANDRE PEPIN--Age 25, of La Trinite in Normandy, 5'2",
    black hair, laborer.

RENE JEAN--Age 52, of Paris, 5', grey hair, goldsmith
or silversmith.

PIERRE BONBIER--Age 19, of St. Germain la Valle, 5'2",
auburn hair.

Deserters coming from Bayonne by order of

Monsieur le Marechal de Berwick

NICOLAS GIRARD--Age 30, of Calais, 5'4", auburn hair.

JOACHIM LA ROQUE--Age 36, of Lyon, 4'10", black hair.

June 1, 1720--La Rochelle

DESCRIPTIONS OF THE SOLDIERS OF THE NEW
RECRUITMENT WHO EMBARKED ON THE SHIP
LE PROFOND, COMMANDED BY MONSIEUR DU-
GUERMEUR DE PEMANECH, DESTINED TO SERVE
THE COMPANY OF THE INDIES IN
LOUISIANA.

Cadets

PIERRE PERON DE LA CUREE--Age 23, of Issoudun, 4'8",
blond hair.

THOMAS BERNARD ROBILLARD DE BEAUREPAIRE--Age 20, of Caen,
5', brown hair.

Sergeant

CLAUDE MARECHAL--Age 39, native of Moulins in Bourbonois,
5', black hair, sent from Paris.

Soldiers

FRANCOIS FERTEL--Age 18, of Corby in Picardy, 4'10", black
hair, baker.

JULIEN MAGDELEINE--Age 20, of Rennes in Bretagne, 5',
          auburn hair, surgeon (<u>chirurgien</u>).

LOUIS GAU--Age 17, of Tours, 4'8", black hair, worker in
          silk.

PIERRE BORGNE--Age 26, of Troyes in Champagne, 5', black
          hair, dyer.

JEAN ROUSSEL--Age 15, of Vannes in Bretagne, 4'8", black
          hair.

PIERRE VAUGOIS--Age 18, of Rennes in Bretagne, 4'4",
          black hair, barber of wig-maker.

LOUIS MENARD--Age 35, of Longueville in Poitou, 4'10",
          black hair, butcher.

ETIENNE EUGUENAIN--Age 16, of Macon, 5', black hair,
          carpenter.

ANTOINE LA ROCHE--Age 20, of Macon, 5', auburn hair,
          weaver.

PIERRE POUSSINE--Age 14, of Monbart in Bourgogne, 4'6",
          auburn hair, tailor.

ANTOINE LEGROS--Age 20, of Moulin, 5'3", auburn hair,
hosier.

NICOLAS OHIER--Age 22, of Abbeville, 5', auburn.

NICOLAS THIBAULT--Age 16, of Clermont in Auvergne, 4',
auburn hair, shoe-maker.

CLAUDE REY--Age 40, of Cie in Charolais, 5'4", black
hair, shoe-maker.

JEAN BAPTISTE CONMOLET--Age 20, of Cay-la (sic with
hyphen) in Languedoc, 5', blond hair.

JACQUES BENARD--Age 36, of Angers, 5'2", black hair,
ship's carpenter.

ANTOINE GRIMAL--Age 30, of Aurleac (or Aurbac) in Auvergne,
5', black hair, shoe-maker.

CLAUDE PERRON--Age 20, of St. Etienne de Riz, 5', black
hair.

NICOLAS RIGOLET--Age 16, of Lyon, 5', auburn hair.

PIERRE CALLET--Age 20, of Lyon, 5', auburn hair.

HENRY THOMAS--Age 21, of Chalons, 5', auburn, expert
    seaman.

JEAN LOUIS DUPAIN--Age 18, of Bourg in Bresse, 5'1",
    black hair, weaver.

JEAN SIMONET--Age 21, of Chateau Regnault in Tourenne,
    5', black hair, carder or wool-comber.

CLAUDE PARROU--Age 25, of Marsonnat in Bresse, 5'1",
    auburn hair, laborer.

AYME BRULE--Age 23, of Marsonnat in Bresse, 5', auburn
    hair.

July 15, 1720

DESCRIPTIONS OF THE SOLDIERS OF THE NEW
RECRUITMENT IN THE   SERVICE   OF THE COM-
PANY OF THE INDIES WHO EMBARKED ON THE
FLUTE MARIE, COMMANDED BY MONSIEUR DE
PONT LO, HAVING LEFT FOR THE SAID COLONY
(OF LOUISIANA) 15 JULY 1720.

Cadets

The Sieurs:

DANIEL DE MEURLY--Age 28, of St. Gal in Switzerland, 5',
auburn hair.

NICOLAS CHAZELLE--Age 40, of Paris, 5'3", brown hair.

JACQUES DURCET--Age 25, of St. Jacques Dillier in Bausse,
4'10", black hair, sent from Paris.

JOSEPH DE L'ISLE--Age 15, of St. Sulpice, black hair.

FRANCOIS MAISONNEUVE--Age 30, of Blois, 5', black hair.

LOUIS RIBERT--Age 17, of Versailles, 5', black hair.

44

Sergeants

The _Sieurs_:

LOUIS HEBERT--Age 48, of Rouen, 5', auburn hair, cooper
        sent from Paris.

JACQUES PREVILLE--Age 28, of Ste. Heleine in Savoye, 5'4",
        black hair.

Soldiers

JACQUES BONEAU--Age 18, of Autun, 5', black hair, tanner.

LOUIS LIONSEL--Age 23, of Coudon in Xaintonge, 5'1",
        "_clair._"

BERNARD DUFOUR--Age 31, of Bergerac in Perigord, 4'10",
        black hair, hosier.

MATHURIN DE LA TOUCHE--Age 26, of Plomene in the bishopric
        of St. Malo, 4'10", black hair, weaver.

PIERRE BERNARD--Age 18, of Rufay in Poitou, 5', black
        hair, laborer.

YVES JOSEPH LE DELIVRE--Age 35, of Carhaix in the bishopric
        of Quimpert, 5'2", brown hair.

LOUIS LESDIGUIERE--Age 45, of Abbeville in Picardy, 5',
        brown hair, gardener.

PIERRE FLEURTET--Age 18, of Gergy near Chalons, 5',
        auburn hair, wheelwright.

NICOLAS ST. MICHEL--Age 25, of St. Germain in Laye, 4'10",
        brown hair, surgeon (chirurgien).

JACQUES DESJARDINS--Age 40, of Chomotel, 5', black hair,
        gardener.

ETIENNE LENORMAND--Age 36, of Orleans, 5', black hair,
        cooper.

JEAN BAPTISTE PIERRE--Age 23, of Frainay in Champagne,
        5', black hair, barber or wig-maker.

BASTIEN FROIN--Age 30, of Mauze, 5'1", black hair.

RENE FOUCAUD--Age 40, of Niort, 5'3", black hair, shoe-
        maker.

JEAN BOYER--Age 25, of Ardam in Poitou, 5', black hair.

JEAN FOURNIER--Age 31, of Angouleme, 5'2", auburn hair.

PHILIPPE POUPART--Age 23, of Allencon in Normandy, 5',
        black hair, carder or wool-comber.

JEAN CHANFAILLY--Age 23, of Allencon in Normandy, 5',
        black hair, potter (potier de terre).

PIERRE GARREAU--Age 16, of St. Andre in Poitou, black
        hair.

NICOLAS VINCONNEAU--Age 15, of Seche in Anjou, 4'7",
        auburn hair, laborer.

PIERRE MATHIEU DURIN--Age 45, of Marle in Picardy, 5'6",
        auburn hair.

CLAUDE FONTAINE--Age 37, of St. Germain in Laye, 5', auburn
        hair, laborer.

JULIEN HUBERT--Age 26, of Dol in Bretagne, 5', auburn
        hair, laborer.

JOSEPH DUCROS--Age 27, of Toulouse, 5', auburn hair,
        laborer.

PIERRE BOUCOUD--Age 17, of Richelieu in Poitou, 4'8",
        blond hair.

JEAN GRIVOIS--Age 36, of Villaire in Picardy, 5'1",
    black hair.

JACQUES MEMANTEAU--Age 28, of La Gore near La Rochelle,
    5', black hair, laborer.

FRANCOIS GILLE--Age 36, of Clerc in Touraine, 5', auburn
    hair, laborer.

FRANCOIS BAZILLE--Age 22, of Auxerre in Bourgogne, 5',
    black hair, cooper.

LOUIS LOPINOT--Age 14, of Canada, black hair.

RENE BULOIN--Age 22, of Flemier(?) near Angers, 4'8",
    black hair.

RENE HERY--Age 16, of Angers, 4'8", black hair.

ISRAEL BASOURDY--Age 45, of Loudun, 5', black hair.

BLAIZE RENOULEAU--Age 22, of St. Martin in Xaintonge, 5',
    black hair, laborer.

BLAIZE ARNOULT--Age 21, of Paris, 5', auburn hair, laborer.

NICOLAS PICAULT--Age 19, of Orleans, 4'8", black hair,
        joiner or carpenter.

SIMON GOUANOT--Age 25, of Giron near Bordeaux, 5', black
        hair.

FRANCOIS ROULEAU--Age 23, of Rennes in Bretagne, 4'9", black
        hair, weaver.

ANTOINE SINAIS--Age 17, of Millen near Bordeaux, 5',
        black hair, laborer.

JEAN METIVIER--Age 21, of La Chapelle Blanche, 4'10",
        black hair, laborer.

JEAN FULMY--Age 18, of Belislle(?) in Poitou, 5', black
        hair, butcher.

ANTOINE DOMINIQUE--Age 28, of Rouanne near Lyon, 4'10",
        black hair, clothes tailor (tailleur
        d'habits).

LOUIS YSAC DUCOUDRAY--Age 30, of Genevre, 5', brown hair,
        shoe-maker.

JACQUES NOVET--Age 35, of Boguicy, 5', black hair,
        laborer.

JEAN FALIGAN--Age 34, of Argenton <u>les Englises</u> in the
diocese of Poitou, <u>5'2"</u>, black hair.

JEAN DIMIER--Age 21, of Chateauneuf in Angoumois, 5',
black hair, weaver.

FRANCOIS FERRET--Age 20, of Rennes in Bretagne, 5', black
hair, tailor.

CLAUDE ARNOULT--Age 30, of Besancon in Franche Comte,
5', black hair, tailor.

JEAN JACQUES--Age 37, of Langon near Bordeaux, 5'2",
black hair.

JACQUES BERTAUDOT--Age 16, of Addam in Poitou, 4'10",
auburn hair, laborer.

JACQUES ROBERT--Age 33, of Sel in Poitou, 5'6", black
hair, shoe-maker.

JEAN YVONNET--Age 21, of Chateau Regnault in Tourenne,
5', black hair, carder or wool-comber.

JEAN FORT--Age 30, of St. Dony near Bordeaux, 5', black
hair, surgeon (<u>chirurgien</u>).

JEAN CASSERAND--Age 20, of Givere in Bearn, 5', auburn
          hair, cook.

LOUIS GODINEAU--Age 29, of St. Pierre Achain near Tours,
          4'10", auburn hair, laborer.

LOUIS ANTOINE ROLLAND--Age 26, of Orleans, 5', auburn
          hair, glover.

MICHEL MINCE--Age 20, of the parish of St. Severin in the
          bishopric of Blois, 5'1", black hair,
          laborer.

PHILBERT BONFANDEAU--Age 17, of Barbeziere, 5', black
          hair, laborer.

JOSEPH PIZENAC--Age 20, of Autun, 5', black hair.

GUILLAUME BODINEAU--Age 20, of Paray, 5', black hair.

MARTIN FLEUR--Age 21, of Paray, 5', black hair.

JEAN MARCOU--Age 19, of the parish of St. Victor-sur-
          Loire, 5', blond hair, ribbon-maker or
          ribbon-vender.

JEAN BAPTISTE BREDA--Age 18, of Mons, 5', black hair.

CLAUDE CORNET--Age 20, of Mons, 5', black hair.

FRANCOIS DUFOUR--Age 32, of Paris, 5', black hair, shoe-
maker.

CLAUDE BERTRAND--Age 17, of Grenoble, 5', auburn hair.

NICOLAS MANDERLIER--Age 22, of St. Jullien, 5'2", black
hair, shoe-maker.

LUC THIBAUD--Age 18, of St. Jullien, 4'10", black hair.

FRANCOIS FRAINE--Age 18, of Corby in Picardy, 4'10",
black hair, baker.

HUBERT LE BLANC--Age 25, of St. Brun, 5'1", black hair,
laborer.

FRANCOIS LA BOISSIERE--Age 21, of St. Brun, 5', black
hair.

JEAN DAVID--Age 18, of Macon, 5', auburn hair, shoe-maker.

PIERRE MAILLE--Age 20, of Macon, 5', auburn hair.

GUILLAUME DARGENTEL--Age 18, of the bourg of La Clayette,
    5', auburn hair, tailor.

CLAUDE PERRIN--Age 25, of Serigny, 5', auburn hair, shoe-
    maker.

PIERRE MAIN--Age 40, of Chef Bouton in Poitou, 5'1",
    black hair, gardener.

FRANCOIS DURCY--Age 23, of Bordeaux, 5', auburn hair,
    brazier or coopersmith.

PIERRE SAMSON--Age 35, of Abbeville in Picardy, 5',
    black hair, cook.

PIERRE GASSAGNE--Age 25, of Chamac in Languèdoc, 6',
    black hair.

GLOSSARY

Spellings used in the original documents
are retained.

Armurier--armourer, gunsmith.

Barbier--barber.

Blond--blond.

Bonnetier--hosier.

Boucher--butcher.

Boulanger--baker.

Boutonnier--button-maker.

Broissier--probably <u>brossier</u>--brush-maker, brush-seller.

Cadet--cadet.

Cardeur--carder, wool-comber.

Chappellier--hatter.

Charpentier--carpenter, ship-carpenter.

Chartier--probably <u>charretier</u>--carter, waggoner.

Chatain--auburn.

Chaudronnier--brazier, coopersmith, tinker.

Cordonnier--shoe-maker.

Cuisinier--cook.

Drapier--draper, clothier.

Fondeur--founder, caster, smelter.

Flute--large, narrow-sterned Dutch cargo-boat.

Forgeron--blacksmith, smith.

Fratter--possibly _freteur_--freighter or charterer.

Gantier--glover.

Imprimeur--printer.

Jardinier--gardener.

Laboureur--laborer.

Lanternier--lantern-maker or lamplighter.

Lunetier--spectacle-maker, spectacle-seller.

Manoeuvrier--expert seaman.

Marechal--marshal.

Masson--mason.

Matelot--sailor.

Menuissier--carpenter.

Merain--probably _merrain_--stave-wood, clap-board, beam
              (or deer horn).

Meunier--miller.

Mineur--miner.

Navire--vessel, ship.

Noir--black.

Roux--reddish.

Orfevre--goldsmith or silversmith.

Ouvrier en soye--silk worker.

Parfumeur--perfumer.

Patissier--pastry-cook.

Paveur--pavior.

Perruquier--barber, wig-maker.

Potier de terre--potter.

Serrurier--lock-smith or metal worker.

Tailleur--tailor.

Tanneur--tanner.

Tinturier--teinturier--dyer.

Tisserant--weaver.

Tonnelier--cooper.

Tourneur--turner.

Vaizzeau--vessel.

Vigneron--vine-dresser, wine-grower.

INDEX OF PERSONAL NAMES

Bataillon. See George, Jean

Baudet, Francois, called Bastillon, 33

Bazille, Francois, 48

Beau, Michel, 12

Beaulieu. See Pasquier, Andre

Beaumenal, 4

Beaurepas, Zacharie, 22

Beausejour. See Despace, Jean

Beauvois, Jean, 9

Bellair, Jacque Brigond, 13

Bellamy, Charles, 25

Bellar, Louis, 27

Belle Fleur. See Medieu, Antoine

Benard, Jacques, 42

Bernard, Claude, called Chambery, 38; Pierre, 45

Benoist, Claude, 11

Berson, Ennemond, 37

Bertaudot, Jacques, 50

Berthelot, Francois, called Marais, 38

Bertrand, Claude, 52

Beuret, Jean Guillaume, 23

Besuchet, Pierre, 29

Bideau de St. Jacques, Pierre, 21

Billecault, Francois, 30

Billieux. See Courbinet de Billieux

Blanchard, Louis, 34

Bleret, Nicolas, 10

Blochet, Louis, 34

Bodineau, Guillaume, 51

Boid, Jean, 14

Boiledieu, Louis Raymond, 12

Bolle, Ignace de, 15

Bonbier, Pierre, 39

Boneau, Jacques, 45

Bonfandeau, Philbert, 51

Bonger, Jean Pierre, 13

Bonnemens. See Girault, Francois

Bonteau, Pierre, 25

Bontems, Charles, 8

Boquet, Jean Baptiste, 12

Borgne, Pierre, 41

Bouchet, Jacques, 33

Boucoud, Pierre, 47

Boyer, Jean, 46

Branchet, Michel, 38

Brat, Jean, 36

Brau, Jean Baptiste, 13

Breau, Nicolas, 31

Breda, Jean Baptiste, 52

Brindonneau, Rene, 24

59

Bringuan, Nicolas, 18

Brule, Ayme, 43

Brunet, Jean, 5, 31

Buffet, Francois, 15

Buffy, Jean, 9

Buloin, Rene, 48

Calet, Charles, 31

Callery, Jacques, 15

Camuzat, Pierre, 2

Capitaine, Adrien le, 19

Carlier, 4

Casmier, Charles, 5

Casserand, Jean, 51

Catinoy, Francois, 2

Caze, Germain, 25

Chambery. _See_ Bernard, Claude

Chanfailly, Jean, 47

Chapelle, Guillaume, 32

Charles, Jean, 27

Charpentier, Francois, 12

Chavannes, 16

Chazelle, Nicolas, 44

Chechery, Jean, 25

Chenay, Jean, 26

Cheron, Francois, 37; Robert, 19

Chery, Maurice, 21

Cheuveier, Jacques, 19

Chevalier. _See_ Laurendicq, Pierre

Clarasky, Georges, called La Violette, 13

Claude de la Couze, Jean, 21

Claude, Joachim, called Sans Facon, 21

Clautier, Jean, 10

Clery, Joseph, called Sansoucy, 7

Collet, Pierre, 42

Colloin, Jean, 36

Conmolet, Jean Baptiste, 42

Cornet, Claude, 52

Coucou. _See_ Quinau

Coulau, Monsieur, 28

Coulombier, Monsieur Du, 1

Courbinet de Billieux, 6

Couttant, Francois, 36

Crevecoeur, Elzear Felix de, 29

Crolies, Charles, 20

Cussin, Pierre, 36

Darbet, Francois, 6

Darbanne, 17

Dargentel, Guillaume, 53

Dauges, Louis, called La Sonde, 24

Daunin, Jean, 35

Du Fourg, 18

Duguermeur de Pemanech, Monsieur, 40

Duhamel, Francois Nicolas, 5

DuMont, Francois, 11; Louis, 10

Dupain, Jean Louis, 43; Louis, 11

Durand, Antoine, 7

Durcet, Jacques, 44

Durcy, Francois, 53

Durin, Pierre Mathieu, 47

Du Pre, Jean, 30, 33; Thomas, 34

du Rocher, Rene, 30

Du Val, Charles, 30; Claude, 20

Euguenain, Etienne, 41

Evenan, Ollivier, 5

Evrard, Jean Baptiste, 2

Faligan, Jean, 50

Famechon, Louis Nicolas, 33

Fausset, Pierre, 38

Ferrand, Jean Baptiste, 26; Laurens, 37

Ferret, Francois, 50

Fertel, Francois, 40

Feuillee, Monsieur de la, 4

Flerieux, Nicolas, 11

Fleur, Martin, 51

Fleurtet, Pierre, 46

Fleury, Antoine, 38

Flos, Pierre Antoine du, 28

Fonquerolle, Philippe, 1

Fontaine, Claude, 47

Fort, Jean, 50

Fortier de Beaulier, Claude, 23

Foucaud, Rene, 46

Fouquet, Simon, 3

Fournier, Jean, 46

Fraine, Francois, 52

Frementier, Jean Francois, 31

Fresinet, Pierre, 1

Frocour, Jean, 32

Froget, Vincent, called Pied de Chat, 34

Froin, Bastien, 46

Fulmy, Jean, 49

Fuyer, Pierre, 4

Gabriel, Antoine, called La Forest, 23

Garnier, 8

Garreau, Pierre, 47

Gassagne, Pierre, 53

Gau, Louis, 41

Gaultier, Rene, 12

Gentil, Francois, 12; Jacques, 32; Jean, 9

Geoffroy, Hyacinthe, called Provencal, 20

George, Jean, called Bataillon, 21

Gerre de la Villette, Antoine, 15

Giberty, 8

Gille, Francois, 48

Girard, Nicolas, 39

Girault, Francois, called Bonnemens, 31

Glaine, Claude, 33

Gobet, Pierre, 19

Godineau, Louis, 51

Gottard, Jean, 37

Gottefrin, Jean, 34

Gouanot, Simon, 49

Gouet, Denis, 29; Jacques, 30

Gouin, Claude, 20

Grandin de St. Louis, Barthelemy, 22

Grave, Monsieur de la Manseliere, 17

Grimal, Antoine, 42

Grivois, Jean, 48

Grondin, Michel, 24

Guay, Jean, 7

Guerard, Pierre, 26

Guerin, 8

Guernel, Louis, 36

Guillaume, Claude, 25; Jean, 25

Guillory, Jean, 26

Hafy. See Hassy, Fleury

Hassy, Fleury, 6

Haye, Robert de la, 11

Hebert, Louis, 45

Henault, Jean, 4

Henry, Pierre, 5

Hermies, La Mothe, 4

Hermiet. See Hermies, La Mothe

Heroux, Pierre, 18

Hery, Rene, 48

Higuet, Daniel, 14

Hingler, Gaspard, 21

Hobreman, Panerasse, 13

Hocart, Pierre, 5

Hubert, Jean, 1; Julien, 47

Jacques, Jean, 50

Jamin, Pierre, 18

Japye, Monsieur, 8

Jardin, Alexis du, 32

Jarry, Jean Baptiste, 14

Jean, Rene, 39

Jeune, Jacques, called Baguette, 22

Jollin, Jean, 11

Joman. See Jonnan, Joseph

Jonnan, Joseph, 2

Jordan, Antoine, 28

Josse, Francois Antoine, 23

Joubart, 6

Jounan. See Jonnan, Joseph

Jouneau, Andre, 1

Jounnas, Joseph, 37

Joussaint, Nicolas, called La Bonte, 20

Jus, Robert, 27

La Boissiere, Francois, 52

La Cour, Charles, 27

Ladner, Christian, 15

La Forest. See Gabriel, Antoine

La Haye, Barthelemy de, 10

Laisne, Simon, 24

Lambert, Jacques, 35

Lameron, Jacques, 27

La Mothe, Pierre, 10

Langlois, Jean Almesse de, 22

La Prudence. See Salouin, Mathieu

La Rize. See Deschamps, Joseph

La Roche, Antoine, 41; Jacques, 28

La Roque, Joachim, 39

La Sonde. See Dauges, Louis

Launoy, Jean, 25

Laurendica, Pierre, called Chevalier, 12

La Varette, 3

Lavenot, Jean, 7

La Vergne, Jean, 19

La Vigne, 2

La Violette. See Clarasky, Georges, and Vigneron,
  Jean Francois

Le Blanc, Hubert, 52

Le Bourgeois, Jacques, 14

Le Breton, Nicolas, 14

Le Coq, Jean, 5

Le Court, Rene, 4

Le De, Francois, 9

Le Gendre, Simon, 3

Legros, Antoine, 42

Le Guerne, Guy, 29

Lemoine, Florent, 30

Lenormand, Etienne, 46

Le Roy, Etienne, 31; Pierre, 11

Lesdiguiere, Louis, 46

Le Tourneur, Pierre, 13

Linger, 32

Lionsel, Louis, 45

Livet, Jacques, 17

Lizeux, Jean, 4

Longchamps, Francois, 14

Lopinot, Louis, 48

Loquet, 18

Lorain, Jacques, 21

Louvroy, Luc du, 1

Louvy, Jean Louis, 19

Magdeleine, Julien, 41

Magny, Pierre, 25

Maillard, Jean, 31

Maille, Pierre, 53

Main, Pierre, 53

Mainnard, Christophe, 10

Mainqueneau, Francois, 31

Maisonneuve, Francois, 44

Malezieux, Etienne, 36

Malsieu, Pierre, 32

Manchet. See Assay, Louis

Manderlier, Nicolas, 52

Marais. See Berthelot, Francois

Marchard, Jean, 11

Marche, Louis La, 11

Marcier, Gerard, 6

Marcou, Jean, 51

Marechal, Claude, 40

Marguet, Jean, 10

Marly, Jean de, 34, 35

Marteau, 20

Marzelle, Jean de la, 31

Massuel, Louis, 33

Matter, Jean Baptiste, 28

Maurix, Pierre, 37

Medieu, Antoine, called Belle Fleur, 22

Meilleray. See Autin, Rene

Memanteau, Jacques, 48

Menard, Louis, 41; Simon, 27

Mercier, Claude, 29

Metayer, Claude, 5

Metivier, Jean, 49

Meurly, Daniel De, 44

Michau, Jean, 1

Michel, 17; Rogues, 10

Michelet, Louis, 12

Michin, Michel, 9

Mince, Michel, 51

Mollard, Jean Baptiste, called Montal, 36

Montal. See Mollard, Jean Baptiste

Montreuil. See Voisin, Pierre

Moreau, Ambroise, 14; Francois, 29

Morisette, 17

Nicolas, Claude, 2

Noiron, Jacques, 35; Michel, 35

Noort. See Noorwegh, Thomas

Noorwegh, Thomas, called Noort, 14

Novet, Jacques, 49

Ohier, Nicolas, 42

Ozanne, Louis, 30

Pallier, Nicolas, 33

Paquet, Jacques, 19

Paquiot, Urbain, 25

Parrou, Claude, 43

Pasquier, Andre, called Beaulieu, 24; Pierre, 13

Passerat, Pierre, 36

Patreu, Francois, 20

Pavils, Pierre, 11

Pepin, Andre, 38

Perdon, Agatte Auge, 30

Perin, Louis, 32

Peron de la Curee, Pierre, 40

Perrin, Claude, 42, 53

Perruchon, Francois, 20

Petit, Claude Antoine, 22

Rigolet, Nicolas, 42

Robert, Jacques, 50

Robillard de Beaurepaire, Thomas Bernard, 40

Robin, Jean, 5; Nicolas, 20

Roche, Louis de, 32

Rolland, Louis Antoine, 51

Rospasser, Martin, 23

Rouanne, Jacques, 6

Rouleau, Francois, 49

Roussel, Claude, 29; Jean, 41; Louis, 37

Rousselet, Joseph, 3; Vincent Michel, 3

St. Amant, Benoist Monder, 13

St. Fronlly, Albert de, 15

St. Michel, Nicolas, 46; Pierre Leonnard de, 21

St. Olive. See de Haut, Philippe

Sainton, the elder, 17; the younger, 17

Salomon, Louis, 19

Salouin, Mathieu, called La Prudence, 24

Samson, Pierre, 53

Sandra, 18

Sans Facon. See Claude, Joachim

Sanson de la Grange, Jean, 14

Sansot, Jullien, 16

Sansoucy. See Clery, Joseph

Sansquartier. See Thibaud, Pierre Francois

Sans Regret. See Renault, Jean

Saultier, Dey, 18

Saussie, Francois, 26

Senouche, Pierre, 27

Silar, Gaspard, 23

Simonet, Jean, 43; Pierre, 5

Sinais, Antoine, 49

Soret, Pierre, 10

Soubaygné, Jean, 38

Soyer, Francois, 8

Starusquy, Vincelle, 22

Stelly, Simon, 15

Sterling, Philippe, 13

Stocly, Gaspard, 21

Tartre, Claude du, 37

Tesson, Georges, 35

Therasse, Louis Vincent, called Poittevin, 22

Thibaud, Luc, 52; Pierre Francois, called Sansquartier, 23

Thibault, Nicolas, 42

Thomas, Henry, 43; Silvain, 38

Tilloy, Claude, 28

Touche, Mathurin de la, 45

Toussiger, Estienne, 27

Tranchemontagne, 3

Tringuar, Jean Baptiste, 34

Usquain, Georges, 18

Valetin, Claude Audin, 6

Vallet, Nicolas, 26

Valtre, Gerard, 23

Vau, Bernard de, 35

Vaugois, Pierre, 41

Veillon, Benoist Etienne, 37

Venier, Jean, 27

Verdure, Adron, 34

Vernay, Jean, 27

Vigneron, Jean Francois, called La Violette, 14

Vincent, 8

Vinconneau, Nicolas, 47

Villain, Jacques le, _Sieur_ de Beaumenal, 4

Vistard, Edme, 9

Voisin, Pierre, called Montreuil, 24

Volart, Charles, 9

Voysin, Pierre, 29

Yvonnet, Jean, 50

Nancy, 29
Neully, 35
Nevers, 31
Neville in Normandy, 32
Niort, 4, 11, 46
Normandy, 9, 10, 12, 19, 30, 32, 38, 47
Noyars, 14

Orleans, 12, 14, 46, 49, 51
Otratte, 13

Paray, 51
Paris, 3, 5, 6, 8, 9, 10, 14, 15, 16, 17, 18, 19, 20, 23, 24,
    25, 27, 28, 29, 31, 32, 35, 36, 39, 44, 45, 48, 52
Passy near Paris, 3
Pate in Chartres, 10
Perche, 6
Perigord, 45
Perigordin, 3
Peronne, 1
Picardy, 1, 12, 29, 40, 46, 47, 48, 52, 53
Piege, 12
Pinormiand in Casgone, 2
Pitersene, 15
Plomene in the bishopric of St. Malo, 45
Poissy, 13
Poitiers, 18, 22, 30
Poitou, 1, 3, 10, 11, 12, 17, 32, 33, 41, 45, 46, 47, 49, 50, 53
Pontivy in Bretagne, 5
Preseilly in Touraine, 5
Provence, 2

Quimpert, bishopric of, 45

Reignol, 32
Rennes, 1, 4, 16, 20, 25, 26, 31; in Bretagne, 11, 41, 49, 50
Reont in Poitou, 32, 33
Rheims in Champagne, 11
Rhodon, 36
Richelieu in Poitou, 10, 47
Rilly, 31
Rimar, 35
Riom in Auvergne, 19
Rochefort, 9, 30
Rouanne near Lyon, 49
Rouen, 2, 16, 19, 20, 24, 45
Roy in Champagne, 13
Rufay in Poitou, 45

Saine in Poitou, 11
St. Andre in Poitou, 47
St. Antony, 3
St. Benoist-sur-Loire, 38
St. Brieux in Bretagne, 9, 20
St. Brun, 52
St. Clerneus, 23
St. Cloud, 8
St. Donnatien parish in Paris, 5